W9-AYQ-950

Clifton Park - Halfmoon Public Library
475 Moe Road
Clifton Park, New York 12065

The Life of
Florence Nightingale

By Kathleen Connors

Gareth Stevens
Publishing

Please visit our website, www.garethstevens.com. For a free color catalog of all our high-quality books, call toll free 1-800-542-2595 or fax 1-877-542-2596.

Library of Congress Cataloging-in-Publication Data

Connors, Kathleen.
Florence Nightingale / by Kathleen Connors.
 p. cm. — (Famous lives)
Includes index.
ISBN 978-1-4824-0408-1 (pbk.)
ISBN 978-1-4824-0410-4 (6-pack)
ISBN 978-1-4824-0405-0 (library binding)
1. Nightingale, Florence, — 1820-1910 — Juvenile literature.
2. Nurses — England — Biography — Juvenile literature. I. Connors, Kathleen. II. Title.
RT37.N5 C66 2014
610.73092—dc23

First Edition 4239

First Edition

Published in 2014 by
Gareth Stevens Publishing
111 East 14th Street, Suite 349
New York, NY 10003

Copyright © 2014 Gareth Stevens Publishing

Designer: Nicholas Domiano
Editor: Kristen Rajczak

Photo credits: Cover, p. 1 Sir William Blake Richmond/The Bridgeman Art Library/Getty Images; p. 5 View Pictures/Universal Images Group/Getty Images; p. 7 traveler1116/E+/Getty Images; p. 9 Rischgitz/Hulton Archive/Getty Images; p. 11 Mansell/Time & Life Pictures/Getty Images; pp. 13, 19, 21 Hulton Archive/Getty Images; p. 15 Trelleek/The Bridgeman Art Library/Getty Images; p. 17 After William Simpson/The Bridgeman Art Library/Getty Images.

All rights reserved. No part of this book may be reproduced in any form without permission in writing from the publisher, except by a reviewer.

Printed in the United States of America

CPSIA compliance information: Batch #CW14GS: For further information contact Gareth Stevens, New York, New York at 1-800-542-2595.

Contents

Boldface words appear in the glossary.

Nursing Many to Health

Florence Nightingale is the mother of modern nursing. She **dedicated** her life to **improving** medical care all over the world. Many of her ideas are still in use today!

Smart from the Start

Florence was born in 1820. She was named for the city her parents were visiting at the time—Florence, Italy! During her childhood in England, her father taught her math, history, and many languages.

7

At age 16, Florence decided to become a nurse. Her parents **disapproved**, though she had helped sick family members before. Still, in 1850, Florence went to Germany for nursing training.

Small Changes

Florence learned basic medical skills and how to run a hospital. While in charge of a hospital for women, she worked hard to improve the conditions there. Florence trained other nurses, too.

11

Angel of Crimea

In 1854, Florence led nurses to a war-front hospital. There, soldiers fighting in the **Crimean War** had been receiving poor medical care in dirty conditions. She brought supplies and tried to better their care.

13

Florence dedicated herself to the soldiers and the cleanliness of the hospital **wards**. The men knew her as the "lady with the lamp" because she walked the wards at night, helping anyone who needed it.

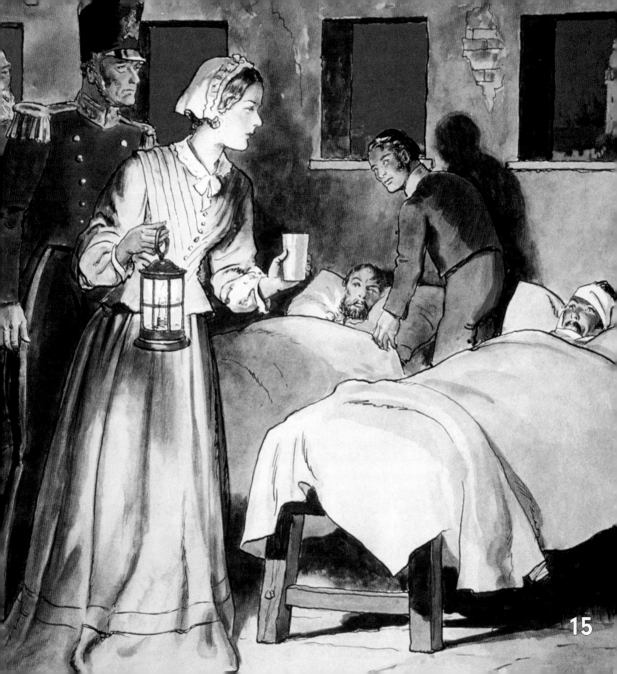

15

Big Changes

Florence wrote about the poor hospital conditions during the war. In 1856, she met with the queen of England to talk about what should be done. Florence's work caused great improvements in the British military.

17

Florence wanted to pass on her ideas. She wrote a book about nursing that was read all over the world. Florence also founded the Nightingale Training School for Nurses in 1860.

Remembered

Even late in life, Florence worked to further nursing training around the world. In 1907, she was the first woman to receive the Order of Merit, an honor given for great service in the armed forces. She died in 1910.

Timeline

1820 — Florence is born.

1850 — Florence starts nursing training.

1854 — Florence begins nursing work during the Crimean War.

1860 — The Nightingale Training School for Nurses opens.

1907 — Florence receives the Order of Merit.

1910 — Florence dies.

Glossary

Crimean War: a war between England and Russia fought from 1853 to 1856. Crimea was the name of an area of Russia at that time.

dedicate: to commit

disapprove: to have an unfavorable view

improve: to make better

ward: a room in a hospital for many patients

For More Information

Books

McCann, Michelle Roehm. *Girls Who Rocked the World: Heroines from Joan of Arc to Mother Teresa.* New York, NY: Aladdin, 2012.

Ridley, Sarah. *Florence Nightingale—and a New Age of Nursing.* Mankato, MN: Sea-to-Sea Publications, 2013.

Websites

Florence Nightingale

www.bbc.co.uk/schools/primaryhistory/famouspeople/ florence_nightingale/
Read all about Florence Nightingale, play a game, and take a quiz about her life.

Florence Nightingale Museum – History

www.florence-nightingale.co.uk/history.html
Learn more about the time period Florence Nightingale lived in on the Florence Nightingale Museum website.

Publisher's note to educators and parents: Our editors have carefully reviewed these websites to ensure that they are suitable for students. Many websites change frequently, however, and we cannot guarantee that a site's future contents will continue to meet our high standards of quality and educational value. Be advised that students should be closely supervised whenever they access the Internet.

Index

JAN 2015

Clifton Park-Halfmoon Public Library, NY

0 00 06 04474239